for

JOEL THE TROLL

Herbert the Timid Dragon

By
Mercer Mayer

Golden Press • New York

Western Publishing Company, Inc.

Racine, Wisconsin

Copyright © 1980 by Mercer Mayer.
All rights reserved. Printed in the U.S.A. by Western Publishing Company, Inc.
No part of this book may be reproduced or copied in any form
without written permission from the publisher.
GOLDEN®, A GOLDEN BOOK®, and GOLDEN PRESS® are trademarks of
Western Publishing Company, Inc.
Library of Congress Catalog Card Number: 80-50986
ISBN 0-307-13732-5

Herbert the dragon lived in a snug cave at the edge of the forest wild. Every night at bedtime, Herbert read a story from his favorite book, KNIGHTS IN ARMOR. He loved the exciting tales of brave knights and princesses in distress.

"I wish I were a brave knight in armor," thought Herbert.

But Herbert wasn't brave. As a matter of fact, Herbert was rather timid. You might even say he was afraid of his own shadow.

Nevertheless, Herbert decided one day to leave home and seek adventure as a knight. He packed his bag and started out along the dusty road.

HERBERT

He hadn't gone far when he came upon a broken-down carriage and a princess in distress. It was just like a story from his favorite book.

"Oh, boy!" thought Herbert. "This is the chance for my first knightly act."

Herbert coughed politely. "May I help?" he asked.

The men fixing the carriage didn't understand
dragon language. What they heard was a terrible
dragon ROAR.

They ran for their lives.

Four bowmen stepped out of the woods. Herbert didn't know they were the princess's royal guard. He thought they were kidnappers. He grabbed the princess to save her. The bowmen began to shoot.

Dragons are too scaly to be hurt by arrows. But Herbert was scared. And whenever Herbert was scared he ran. So Herbert ran and ran and ran....

He ran straight home to his snug cave.

Herbert slammed the front door and bolted it shut. He breathed a sigh of relief.

As for the princess, she began to rant and rave. "Listen, you silly-looking dragon," she shouted, "when my father the king finds out you've carried me away, he's going to cut off your head."

"Oh, my," thought Herbert. "What have I done?"

He opened the door so the princess could leave.

"Oh, no," she said. "My mother told me never to go out alone after dark. I'm staying right here until my father comes to rescue me. You just wait — you're going to get it."

"Perhaps some music will cheer her up,"
thought Herbert. He turned on the radio.
But the princess shouted, "I hate dragon music!"
and broke his radio.

Herbert prepared a great big bowl of soup for
the princess.

"Icky, sticky dragon soup — UGH!" cried the
princess, and she threw it in his face.

Herbert tidied up the guest room and put
clean sheets on the bed.

But the princess shrieked, "Dusty, musty dragon
bed—YUCK!" and tore up the sheets.

Then she threw a temper tantrum. She smashed
all of Herbert's fine dragon-bone china.

She tipped over his bookcase. She tromped on his toys.
The princess carried on all night. Herbert got very little sleep.

In the morning, there came a loud banging
at the door. Poking his head out the window,
Herbert saw a brave knight in armor.

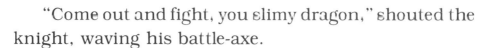

"Come out and fight, you slimy dragon," shouted the knight, waving his battle-axe.

Herbert was frightened. And whenever Herbert was frightened he got the hiccups.

Herbert hiccuped and hiccuped and hiccuped. Billows of smoked poured from his nose.

Needless to say, the brave knight in armor galloped away as fast as he could.

That afternoon, the king and his whole army marched into Herbert's front yard. "I'm going to make mincemeat out of you, oh foul and villainous dragon," shouted the king.

"He couldn't be talking about me," thought Herbert.

One look at the cannon and the battering ram and Herbert was terrified. And whenever Herbert was terrified he began to cough.

Herbert coughed and coughed and coughed. Streams of fire and smoke poured from his nose and mouth. The great cannon melted; the battering ram caught fire. The army panicked and ran away.

"Now look what you've done, you terrible dragon!" said the princess. "You've scared away my father's army."

In a huff she pushed Herbert aside and left, slamming the door behind her.

erbert was broken-hearted. He had certainly made a mess of things. "I guess I'm not cut out to be a brave knight in armor," he thought.

For days Herbert just slunk around his cave, feeling very unpopular. Then a troll friend of his dropped in for a visit.

"Herbert, have you heard the news?" he asked.

Of course, Herbert hadn't. His radio was still broken.

"It's just awful," said the troll. "After you melted down the king's cannon and scattered his army, the evil Duke of Dingbat and his bandits kidnapped the princess and carried her away to the Castle Grouch. And the king has no army to rescue her."

Well, dragons usually have treasure lying around.
And Herbert just happened to have a wagonload of gold
in his cellar at that very moment.

"I will take my gold to the Castle Grouch and ransom
the princess," thought Herbert. "It's the least I can do."

He set off for the Castle Grouch, pulling his wagonload
of gold.

Herbert knocked at the gate of the Castle Grouch.

"Hello," he called. "I'll trade you this wagonload of gold for the princess."

But the Duke of Dingbat didn't understand dragon language. What he heard was a terrible dragon ROAR.

"A dragon has attacked!" he shouted. "Dump a ton of boulders on him. That'll fix his wagon."

So the duke's bandits pushed a ton of boulders off the castle wall, right on top of Herbert.

Of course, Herbert's dragon scales were so thick that he wasn't hurt a bit.

But Herbert was horrified. And whenever Herbert was horrified his nose tickled. And whenever his nose tickled he sneezed.

But our wagon doesn't need fixing.

"Ah-ah-ah-ah-CHOO!!"
Herbert sneezed a great blast that blew a huge hole
in the wall of the Castle Grouch.

You don't have to think very hard to know that the
duke and his bandits tried to slip out the back door.
But the duke had lost his key, so they were trapped.

Herbert took the princess back to her father's castle.
He made the Duke of Dingbat and his bandits pull
the wagonload of gold all the way.

You've probably guessed that Herbert was very
popular, indeed. The king made him First Knight and
Grand Dragon of the Realm.

Then the king gave a big party, with music and dancing and presents for everyone (except the Duke of Dingbat — he had to work on the safety patrol).

Herbert was a knight in armor at last. But not a *brave* knight in armor. Because he was still the same old timid Herbert.

Of course, nobody knew that except the princess. And she never told anyone. However, she always made sure that no one ever scared, frightened, terrified, or horrified Herbert again.

THE END